Smelling

Library of Congress Number: 79-27147

 2 3 4 5 6 7 8 9 0 84 83 82

Printed in the United States of America.

Library of Congress Cataloging in Publication Data

Allington, Richard L
  Smelling.

  (Beginning to learn about)
  SUMMARY: Describes 14 categories of aromas,
including those associated with holidays, cleanliness, and illness.
  1. Smell — Juvenile literature.   2. Smell —
Psychological aspects — Juvenile literature.
[1. Smell] I. Cowles, Kathleen, joint author.
II. Thrun, Rick. III. Title. IV. Series.
QP458.A38   152.1'66   79-27147
ISBN 0-8172-1293-0 lib. bdg.

Richard L. Allington is Associate Professor, Department of Reading,
State University of New York at Albany.
Kathleen Cowles is the author of several picture books.

BEGINNING TO LEARN ABOUT

SMELLING

BY RICHARD L. ALLINGTON, PH.D., • AND KATHLEEN COWLES
ILLUSTRATED BY RICK THRUN

Raintree Childrens Books • Milwaukee • Toronto • Melbourne • London

You smell with your nose.

Take a walk around your house, apartment, school, or neighborhood. Find as many things to smell as you can. This book will show you some of the smells you might find. Can you think of others?

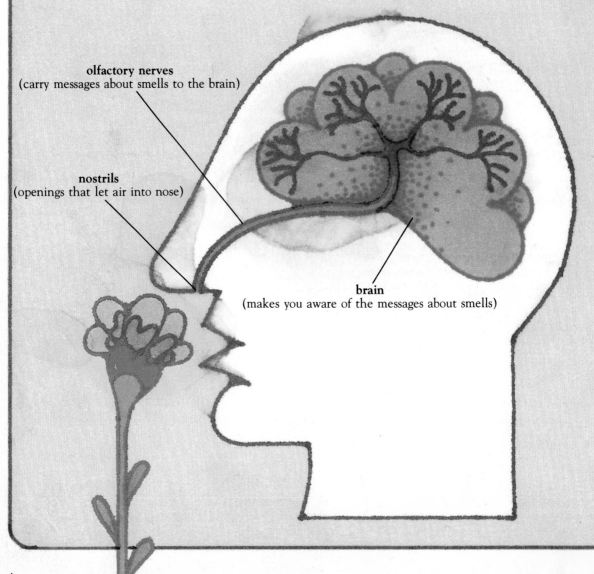

olfactory nerves
(carry messages about smells to the brain)

nostrils
(openings that let air into nose)

brain
(makes you aware of the messages about smells)

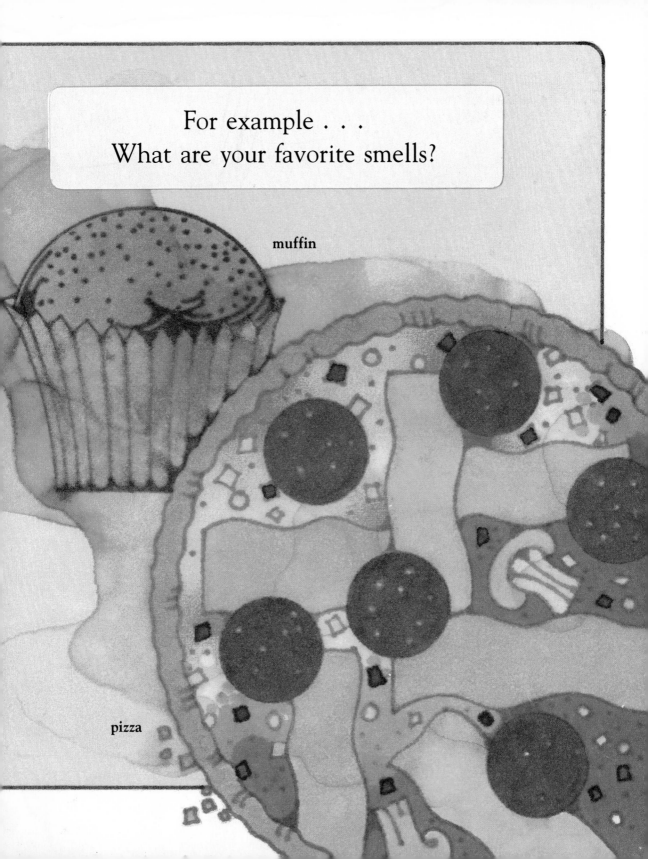

For example . . .
What are your favorite smells?

muffin

pizza

What things make you wish you could smell them all the time?

fresh air

flowers

What things make you wish
you never had to smell them?

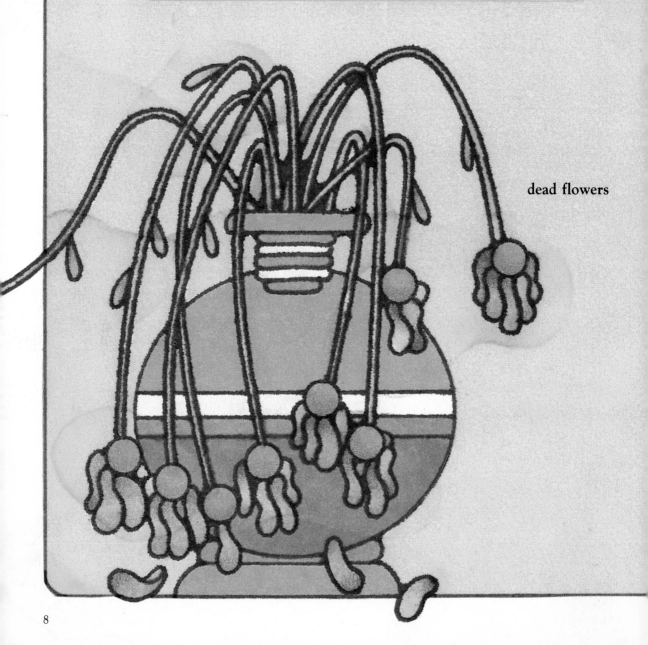

dead flowers

smoggy air

9

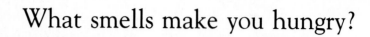

What smells make you hungry?

popcorn

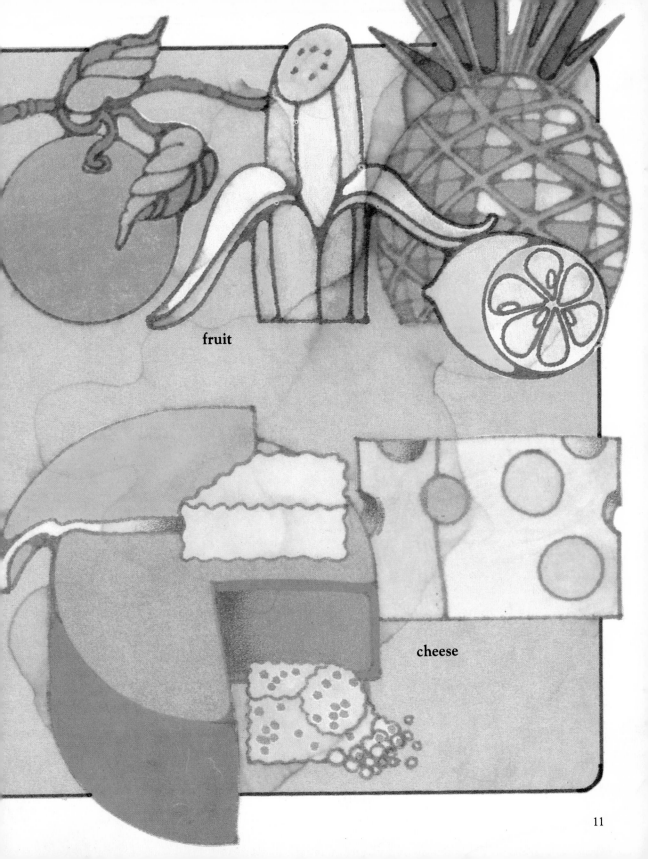

fruit

cheese

11

What smells make you *not* hungry?

sour milk

garbage

birthday cake

14

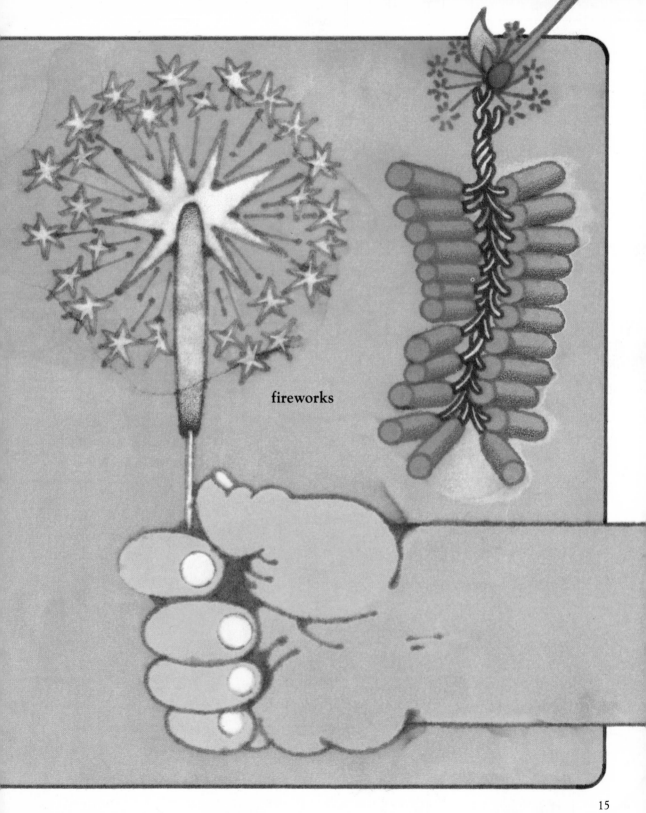

fireworks

What things would you rather
smell than taste?

gum

coffee

What smells make you sneeze
or make your eyes water?

onion

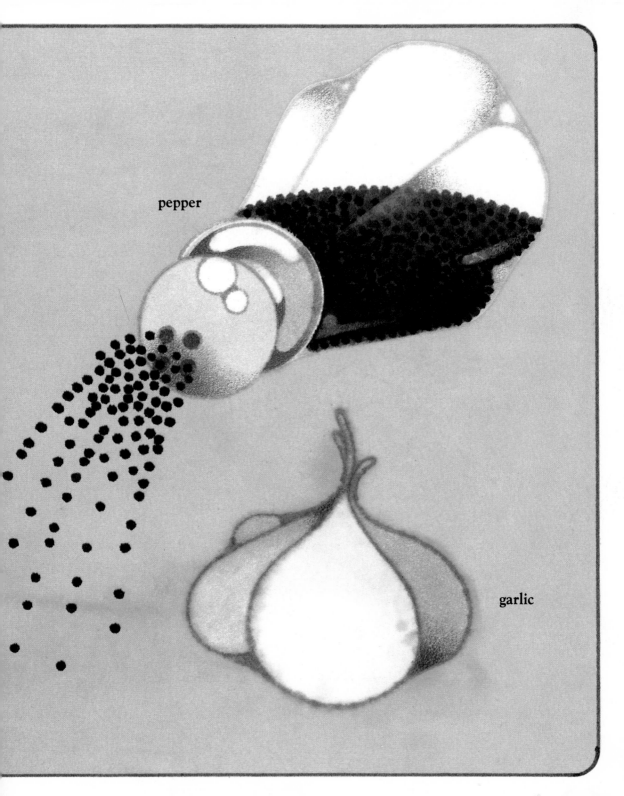

pepper

garlic

19

What smells make you think about being clean?

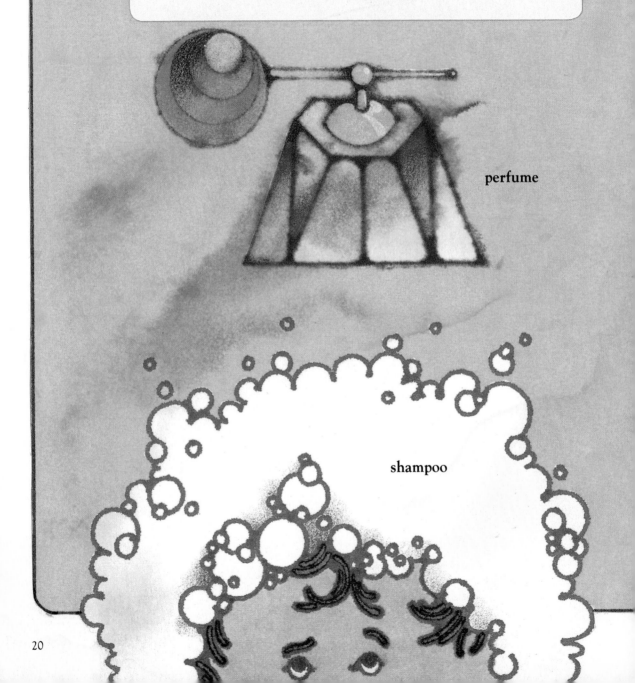

perfume

shampoo

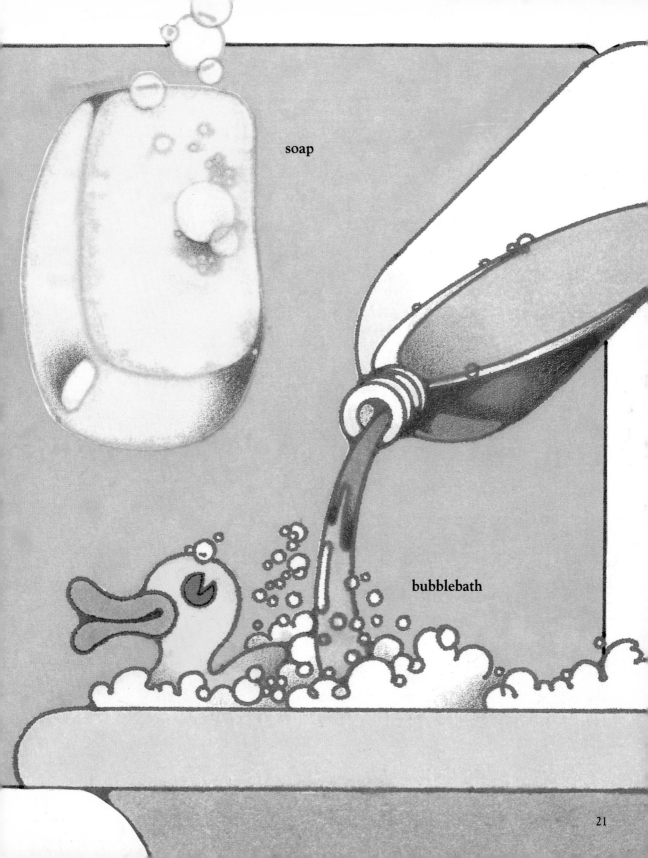

soap

bubblebath

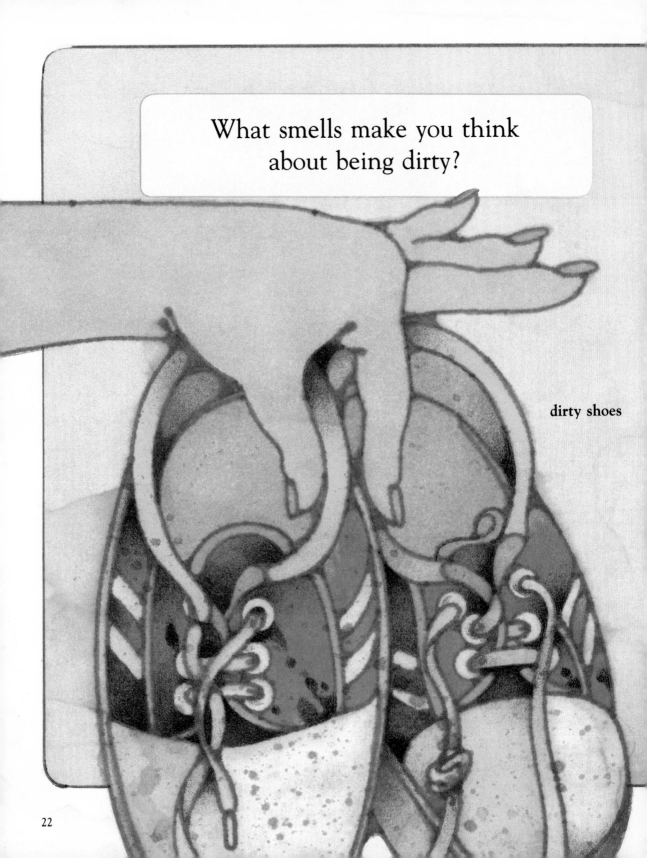

What smells make you think
about being dirty?

dirty shoes

22

sweaty T-shirt

soil

What smells seem to burn your nose?

cigar smoke

24

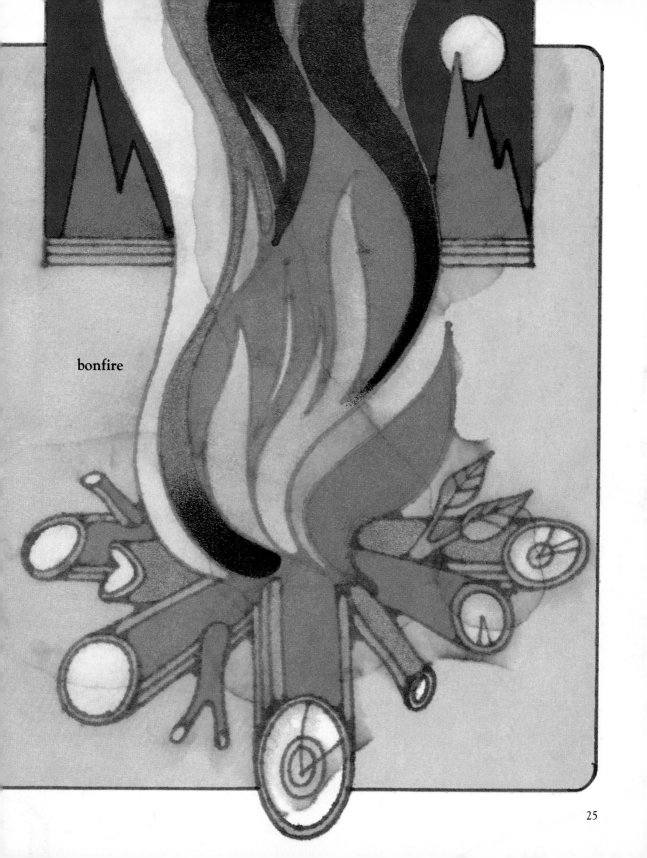

bonfire

25

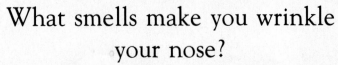

What smells make you wrinkle your nose?

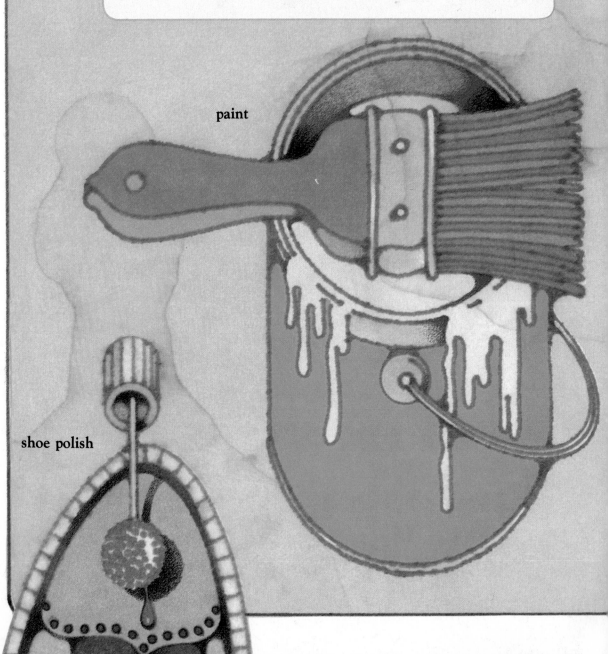

paint

shoe polish

dog

grass

27

What smells make you think
about being sick?

antiseptic

cough drops

iodine

first aid
cream

28

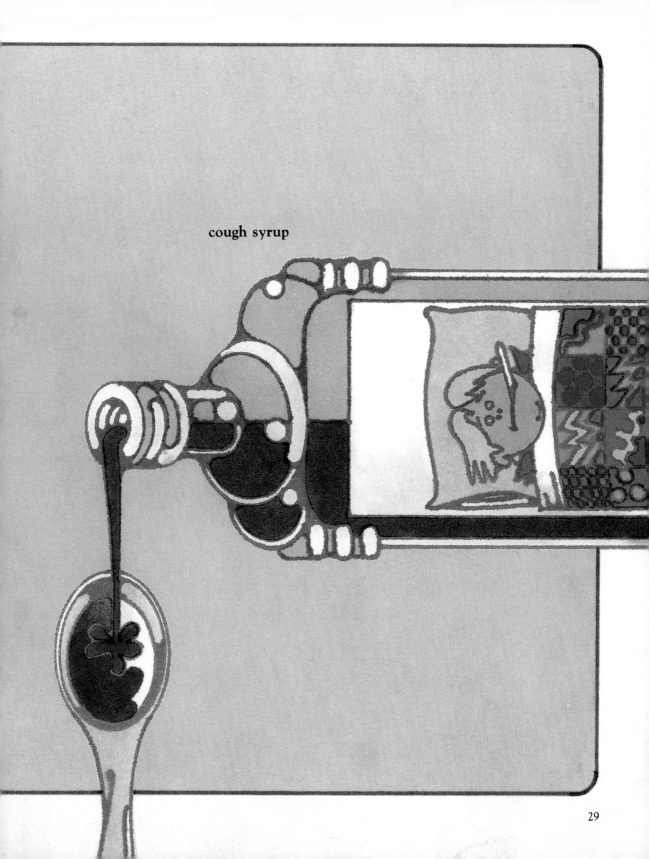

cough syrup

29

What places can you find that have
many things to smell?

cloves

oregano

ginger

vanilla bean

dill

poppy seeds

Find a spice or a flower that you like. Put a spoonful of the spice or of the petals on a small piece of cloth. Tie the ends of the cloth up with ribbon or string. Wear the packet around your neck or wrist. Or put it in the bottom of your clothes drawer.

Take 1 orange and a bottle of whole cloves. Push each clove into the orange as far as it will go. Make 2 circles of cloves around the orange. Tie a ribbon or string around the orange. Hang it up in your room. Or give it to someone as a gift.

Make your own book about smelling. Look through a newspaper or magazine. Find pictures of things you like to smell. Cut out the pictures. Tape or paste them onto pieces of paper. Fasten the papers together. You may ask an adult to help you.